BRINGING YOUR BOOK TO MARKET

A WRITERS' GUIDE TO BECOMING A PUBLISHED

Author

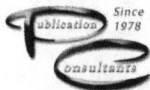

P *Publication* Since 1978 *Consultants*

PO Box 221974 Anchorage, Alaska 99522-1974
books@publicationconsultants.com
www.publicationconsultants.com

ISBN 978-1-59433-347-7
eBook ISBN 978-1-59433-348-4

A Writers' Guide to
Becoming a Published Author

Publication Consultants specializes in publishing the works of writers worldwide. We've been in the publishing business since 1978. We're not only publishers, we're writers, and know many problems confronting writers; how to solve those problems and bring writers' work to market is our business. We welcome this opportunity to become acquainted with you and your work. Many, but not all questions about publishing your book will be answered as you read this booklet. However, after reading Bringing Your Book to Market you will have the basis to ask the right questions when you talk with one of our author representatives.

Although this booklet describes how we bring your book to market, we also work with writers who do not intend to sell their books, but are publishing for self, family, friends, or business purposes. We can publish your book if you don't intend to sell your book, or if you want only a few copies printed—even only one copy.

Publication Consultants produces books and publications of any size, number of pages, and variety of binding and covers. We think there is more to book publishing than just putting ink on paper. Our services include design, typesetting, printing, binding, eBook conversion, and all necessary steps to publish your book, both as a printed book and as an eBook. We take your book from conception to completion and bring your work to market with one of five different programs:

1—Diamond Publishing Program

We assist you in publishing your work. We become your publishing consultant, helping in areas you cannot handle yourself. We do as little or as much as you like. Generally, we take your manuscript and produce a finished printed book and eBook following the steps listed later in this booklet under *Making a Book*. Before we begin, we decide, with you, what you want us to do. We agree on a fee for our services and determine a timeline for their completion. We assist you in decisions about the details of producing your book, such as style, paper, printing, binding, illustrations, and other aspects. We bring the possibilities to you. You make the final decision.

We obtain the copyright for you in your name. The copyright and all subsidiary rights belong exclusively to you. We also obtain a Library of Congress number, UPC code, and ISBN number for your book. These numbers and codes are required for sales of your book to libraries, bookstores, internet, newsstands or eBooks.

Diamond publishing program authors may do their own promoting, marketing, and distributing. If they do their own promoting, marketing, and distributing, they receive all proceeds from the sale of their book, fill all orders, and pay all costs for mailing, shipping, and distribution. However, in addition to their own efforts, most Diamond publishing program authors ask us to handle normal business transactions associated with distribution and help them with marketing. We assist by creating a website in your name (yourname.com), help with your release party, and provide ample opportunities for book signings. We receive all proceeds from the sale of your book, fill all orders, and pay all costs of mailing, shipping, and distribution. You receive regular payments, as per terms of a publishing agreement. Again, we do as little or as much as you want us to do.

2—Ruby Publishing Program

We share the expense of publishing with you— similar to the Diamond publishing program, we take your manuscript and produce a finished printed book and eBook following the steps under *Making a Book*. Before we begin publishing your book, you as the author, and we as the publishers, sign a publishing agreement detailing the terms of our contract. Much the same as the Diamond publishing program, we involve you in the design, layout, and other aspects of producing your book, and in promoting, marketing, and distributing. Details of style, paper, printing, binding, illustrations, time and manner of production, price, publication, and the number of free copies for promotional distribution are agreed on by author and publisher. Again, like the Diamond program, we rely on you as the best marketer of your book. However, we assist by creating a website in your name (yourname.com), help with your release party, and provide ample opportunities for book signings. We supplement, complement, and coordinate your efforts.

We handle all details of obtaining the copyright for you in your name. The copyright belongs exclusively to you. We also obtain the necessary Library of Congress number, UPC code, and ISBN number for your book to be sold to libraries, bookstores, internet, newsstands and eBooks.

Under this program, we handle all normal business transactions associated with marketing your book. We receive all proceeds from the sale of your book, fill all orders, and pay all costs of mailing, shipping, and distribution. You receive regular royalty payments, as per terms of a publishing agreement.

Successful Ruby program authors are involved in marketing their book whether the work has local, regional, or national sales and distributing possibilities.

3—Sapphire Publishing Program

Under this plan, you as the author, and we as the publisher, sign a publishing agreement detailing the terms of our contract. You furnish us with a copy of your manuscript, and we handle all details of producing and selling your book. We make all decisions as to style, paper, printing, binding, illustrations, time and manner of production, price, publication, and the number of free copies for promotional distribution. You proof and approve the final proof copy before your book goes to press. We handle all details of obtaining the copyright for you in your name. The copyright belongs exclusively to you. We also obtain Library of Congress number, UPC code, and ISBN number for your book so it can be sold through normal distribution channels.

We handle all normal business transactions associated with delivering your book to market; however, we may ask you to appear on radio and television talk shows, attend book autographing sessions, and make public appearances to promote your book. These appearances are voluntary and not part of the publishing agreement. We receive all proceeds from the sale of your book, fill all orders, and pay all costs of mailing, shipping, and distribution. You receive regular royalty payments, as per terms of a publishing agreement.

This plan seems to be best for authors whose budget doesn't allow either the Diamond or Ruby publishing programs.

4—We Buy Your Manuscript Outright

Under this plan, you as the author, and we as the publisher, agree on price and terms of buying your manuscript. You receive a one-time fee, but no future royalty payments. We make all decisions as to style, paper, printing, binding, illustrations, time and manner of production, price, publication, and all other decisions relating to publishing, sales, and marketing of your book. Copyright and all subsidiary rights belong exclusively to Publication Consultants.

This plan seems to be best for authors who want to sell their manuscript for a one-time fee, and don't want further involvement in their book.

5—Consulting

In addition to the four programs to bring your book to market, we also consult with authors about their publishing project. If you need experienced assistance for any writing, printing, marketing, promoting, distributing, or other publishing endeavor, we can help. For example, because of our experience in dealing with printers, we have helped self-publishers select the correct printer, and obtain the right price, paper, and binding for their book. We charge an hourly rate for this service. If you're not sure how to proceed in any area of publishing, or desire only specific information or service, a short session with us may save you hundreds of dollars and wasted effort.

About Publication Consultants

Publication Consultants is an Alaska company. Although our offices are in Anchorage, Alaska (The Air Crossroads of the World) we publish works of authors worldwide. We're experienced in working with authors who do not live nearby and in dealing long-distance with printers and distributors throughout the world. Publication Consultants' office is equipped to do business from great distances. Our staff is experienced in assisting clients we have never met or who have never been to our office. This leaves us uniquely suited to work with authors regardless of where they live.

Owners and operators of Publication Consultants have published a magazine, produced a television show and videos, and hosted a weekly television program and daily call-in radio show. In addition we've been published in national magazines, have written four books, and have published more than 300 books for other authors. We are writers and understand writers and what writers want.

Publication Consultants has published works of poetry, history, fiction, drama, religion, as well as children, literary, and scholarly works, theses, essays, textbooks, workbooks, collections, memoirs, Alaskana, Americana, biographies, autobiographies, family histories, directories, brochures, and catalogs.

Whatever the scope of your work, length of your manuscript, number of copies you want, grade and quality of paper, type of cover, or type of binding, you'll find we have the experience to produce a book you'll be proud of.

We take great pride in our personal, friendly, and helpful service. Your book is not just another job to us—we want you to succeed, and will help you in every way we can. We invite you to contact us about publishing your book.

How to Proceed

The best way to get a complete and accurate idea of how we can help bring your book to market is to let us examine your manuscript. We can receive your manuscript using almost all electronic media including an email attachment. We'll give you a firm quote, and suggest one of our five programs for publishing your book. We give you a decision about publishing your book within 10 days of receipt of your manuscript. You are under no obligation.

Your book receives absolute confidentiality while your manuscript is entrusted to our care. We will not permit others, whom you have not approved, to read your work, nor will we discuss terms of your contract, publication dates, content, or other details about your book with anyone unless you give permission. We may ask to send a copy or portion of your manuscript to a few select people for comment to use as endorsements for book covers or to write a foreword, preface, or introduction. In all cases, we will obtain your approval first. We may also invite you to locate someone to write the foreword and/or endorsements for the back cover.

Your material is returned promptly, whenever you request. We'll be happy to discuss your book and give you an idea of what we can do. We'll give you a firm decision after examining your manuscript.

Secret of Our Low Production Costs

We can handle almost any type of book or publication, with virtually any type of binding or paper stock. We are not printers, but use the services of many printers worldwide. Your book isn't limited to the facilities of one printer. We place your book for printing with the printer who can give the best possible quality at the lowest price. We match your book with the best-qualified printer. Because we're writers ourselves, and publish our own works, we know how important it is to have the right printer.

We maintain a small home office staff with limited expenses. Most of our editing, design, and production staff works from their own offices. This allows us to work with the world's finest book-publishing professionals.

How to Prepare Your Manuscript

We prefer your manuscript, artwork, illustrations, photographs to be submitted using electronic media such as a thumb drive or CD. However, most authors simply attach their manuscript to an email message. Hardcopy in the absence of a electronic file should be typed, double-spaced on one side of 8 1/2-by-11-inch paper. Include page number and book title on each page. If you like, include a "dummy" with the manuscript showing position of headlines, illustrations, photographs, and other artwork. If a dummy is not submitted, we use our own judgment.

Photographs and Artwork

We can use slides, photographs, or scanned images either in color or black and white. If color photographs will be used as black-white photographs in your book, we will convert them to black and white. The same goes for color illustrations. We prefer that artwork and photographs be scanned at 300 dpi and submitted on a CD, thumb drive, or other electronic means.

Once we accept your manuscript for publication we will discuss with you how best to submit your photographs and artwork.

Proofreading

Almost all manuscripts require proofreading. We recommend that you use the services of a professional editor before you submit your manuscript to us. A professionally edited manuscript has a much better chance of being accepted for publishing. Unless you object, your manuscript will be read and corrected by a qualified member of our staff. Spelling, punctuation, sentence structure, and style will be corrected. We change nothing you claim as fact. We may question you and give suggestions about grammar or sentences we feel may be confusing or hard to read or understand. The corrected manuscript will be returned to you for final approval before it is sent to the printer. You'll have ample opportunity to read the proofs, correct errors, and make revisions before printing. We will not send your book to the printer until we have approved all details of your book. After receiving your book from us the printer will furnish us with a printer's proof that you will also have opportunity to approve before your book is printed.

Making a Book

Here are the steps generally taken to make your manuscript into a book:

1. You entrust us with your manuscript and tell us what kind of book you have in mind, how many copies you want, any other information you think will be helpful, and which one of our five publishing programs you think will work best for you.

2. We carefully examine your manuscript and give our suggestions and/or an alternative plan and give you a contract outlining the best proposal, along with your exact costs. We give you a decision about publishing your book within 10 days of receipt of your manuscript. If you are not satisfied for any reason, we'll help you make adjustments or promptly return your manuscript.

3. With your signed contract, if it's not included with your manuscript, we need the following information to obtain your copyright:

 a. Title of book and subtitle, if any

 b. Author's name, as it will appear on the title page

 c. Author's full, legal name, birthplace, citizenship, and legal residence

 d. Name of person or organization to whom copyright shall be issued

4. When you return your signed contract and your deposit, and we have the final electronic copy of your manuscript, we do the following preliminary work:

 a. We proofread and edit your manuscript, make necessary correction suggestions, and send you a copy for approval.

 b. We receive your manuscript back from you with your acceptance or rejection of our editor's suggestions.

 c. We make the necessary adjustments and send you a new proof for approval.

 d. We repeat this process as many times as required until you approve the manuscript and it is exactly the way you want it.

 e. We design your book's cover, title page, and chapter headings; select type style and size, paper quality, weight, and brightness, and handle other necessary details to manufacture your book.

f. If your book is hardbound, we select color and grade of cloth and specify color stamping for your cover.

g. We apply for copyright in your name or the name of the organization you designate.

5. We then take your approved manuscript and prepare it for making a proof copy of your book. We use sophisticated, state-of-the-art, computerized phototypesetting and proofing equipment. Your manuscript and graphics are stored in our computer so we can make changes, revisions, or update your manuscript at any time.

6. We next make a proof copy of your book and give you a copy for your final approval.

7. You return the proof copy with your corrections. We'll make corrections and give you as many proofs as required until you're satisfied that your book is ready for printing. This is the last chance to make changes and corrections without incurring additional expense. Your second deposit is usually due at this time. After we've received your approval we send your book to the printer. If it is necessary for you to make changes on the printer's proof, there will be an additional charge.

8. The printer, following our instructions, makes a color proof of the covers and a proof of your book. The printer sends us the proof and color-proof of the cover for approval and necessary corrections, if any.

9. You receive a copy of both proofs and make necessary corrections. This is not the time to revise or change your book. That should have been done prior to sending it to the printer. The purpose of this proof is to confirm the printer followed our instructions and your book is as we conceived it. Your final deposit is usually due when you return the proofs to us.

10. We make the final corrections and return your book to the printer for manufacture.

11. Concurrent to sending your book to the printer we create an eBook and place it for sale in worldwide distribution.

12. The printer manufactures your book and ships it per instructions. Shipment is most often made by truck, with a few advance copies by air. The books are placed in cartons and cartons are banded on a skid for protection.

13. We apply for and register your own domain name (www.yourname.com), create your own website, establish your blog, and provide training on how to use it and engage in social media marketing.

14. Both publisher and author receive copies of your book, and hopefully you're on your way to fame and fortune.

Archiving Your Work

After your book has been printed, the necessary preparatory items will be stored in anticipation of reprint. Because much of the cost for the initial printing involves preparation, reprints cost less. We also store your files for your book on our computer, and another copy offsite for safety and for updates or revisions for a future edition.

Terms

Our terms for publishing books on either the Diamond or Ruby programs are as follows: one-third down with signed contract, one-third when you return the corrected proof copy with your final approval, and the balance when you return the printer's proof and color proof. These are our only terms for these two publishing programs. We do not publish on open account.

Production Time

Pamphlets, brochures, catalogs, and small, saddle-stitched books can often be produced in four to six weeks. Delivery of hardbound and perfect-bound books takes from 8 to 20 weeks, depending on kind and length of manuscript, number of copies, length of time it takes an author to read, correct, and return proofs, type of binding, and previous commitments. Delivery time may be adjusted to fit your budget. We'll give a firm printing date when you sign the publishing contract.

Caution and Advice

Unless you're a nationally known author, or your manuscript has a high sales potential, a definite outlet, or guaranteed advance sales, we usually recommend a small initial press run for books, although the price per copy drops substantially with larger printings. We don't guarantee, or even imply, that any given book will sell thousands of copies. Any publisher who makes such claims is probably misleading you. Printing 1,000 copies of a book is generally sufficient to test its sales potential. We save the publishing and printing elements after your book has been printed. This allows economical reprints when your book sells more than the original press run.

Our experience tells us the best marketer of a book is usually the author. Any one of our five publishing programs will involve you in marketing your book. We'll do our best to place your book into bookstores, newsstands, supermarkets, the internet, and other outlets. We assist your marketing effort by creating a website in your name (yourname.com), help with your release party, and provide ample opportunities for book signings. You are your book's best salesperson.

What's Next

Thanks for your interest in Publication Consultants. If you have questions not answered in this booklet about book publishing, manufacturing, or distribution, please don't hesitate to contact us. Our relationship with you begins with a complimentary consultation to help you determine the feasibility of bringing your book to market, and the most cost-effective specifications and print run of your book. You may contact us by telephone or fax communication or by email. Our email address and phone numbers are:

Voice (907) 349-2424
Fax (907) 349-2426
email: books@publicationconsultants.com

We consider bringing your book to market the beginning of a long-term relationship, and will do all we can to prove worthy of the trust you place in us.

Our Published Authors Write

No publisher I've had is up to the level of Publication Consultants. Evan Swensen is a hard-working perfectionist. He keeps in constant touch and makes it easy to work with him. Best of all, he has a great capacity for patience and will stand by his responsibilities. Publication Consultants has integrity and is a first-class operation. Sarkis Atamian: *The Bears of Manley*

In 1999, I met with Evan Swensen. After meeting him, I concluded that he was a man whom I could trust with my baby. Evan has helped me to touch the lives of many families across the USA and around the world in a very positive way. If you're looking for a publishing company that is headed by a man of integrity who is ethical and fair in his business practices, then Evan Swensen is your man and Publication Consultants is your company. There's no need to look anywhere else to publish your book. You can relax. You have found a home and family with Evan Swensen and Publication Consultants. Dr. Matthew Johnson: *Family Rules, Parenting with a Plan*

When searching for a publisher for *El Gancho*, I asked God to steer me to an upstanding company. There is no doubt in my mind that He answered my prayer. Mike Travis: *El Gancho* and *Melozi*

I have worked with Evan Swensen and Publication Consultants on all of my books, each of them under completely different circumstances--the first through my then employer and the others by myself. In all cases, Evan has been kind, patient, and more than helpful in getting me through the process. He restored my confidence when I was flailing and he provided direction where his voice of experience could best guide me. He is open to both ideas and suggestion, and works in a true collaboration with his authors. Beyond that, he is honest and reliable. I don't think an author could find a better person to help produce a book that imparts a more polished and professional effect. Evan and Publication Consultants are the best choice for authors who really want a quality product and I could not give them a higher recommendation both as people and as professionals. Marianne Schlegelmilch: *Solo Flite, Raven's Light, Coho Waterboy, Feather from a Stranger, Two Tickets and a Feather,* and *Driftfeather on the Alaska Seas*

I'm proud to be affiliated with Publication Consultants. Dianne Barske: *Two Bears There, Mukluks for Annabelle, and How Do You Say Goodbye To An Elephant?*

We feel so fortunate that we hooked up with Publication Consultants instead of some other company that may or may not have treated us so well. Patti Kilson: *Song of the Raven and Carina*

I am glad to have my book published with Publication Consultants. I frequently recommend them to other would-be authors and they always ask me why. I summarize my feelings by saying, "Evan is honest." Dan Maclean: *Paddling the Yukon*

Publication Consultants made the editing and publishing phase of writing my book both painless and rewarding. Evan Swensen helped make my rough and raw manuscript a readable, professional work. He edited and instructed, always in a constructive and cooperative way. He provided guidance in every stage. Without Publication Consultants, my manuscript would still be lying on the shelf, gathering dust. Ron Walden: *Cinch Knot, Devil's Heart, Ice Blue Eyes,* and *Blue Sky and Green Grass*

Without Evan Swensen and the staff of Publication Consultants of Anchorage, My books would not have been published. I'm grateful for their incomparable professionalism. Carl Douglass: *The Last Phoenix, Saga of a Neurosurgeon: The Young Coyote, Saga of a Neurosurgeon: Anything Goes,* and *All in Jest*

Publication Consultants and Evan Swensen have the professionalism to quickly bring a book to market. They handle all the problems while keeping the author in the loop, helping with proofreading and editing. Their expertise makes for a smooth transition to a finished book. Tom Willard: *Demons of Stony River*

I sent Evan Swensen a manuscript I believed in. Luckily so did he. Remaining approachable through the entire bookmaking process, he took the manuscript and helped turn it into a finished, marketable work. I'll always appreciate Evan's professional attitude and his willingness to guide a greenhorn like me. Mark Otte: *Pray for Justice* and *Hide and Seek*

Evan Swensen not only helped me create *Alaska on the Fly*, but without him there would not have been the experiences to write it. I will be indebted to him always. Dan Heiner: *Alaska on the Fly*

I appreciate the expertise and encouragement I received from Publication Consultants to get *Udder Confusion* published. They're tops on my list for professional editing and integrity. Elverda Lincoln: *Udder Confusion* and *Alaska Animal Antics*

A special thanks is due my friend and publisher, Evan Swensen. His efforts have been of great worth to the coming forth of this work. Without his believing in the value of *Following the Light of Christ into His Presence*, it would still be just a manuscript. John Pontius: *Following the Light of Christ into His Presence*

Publication Consultants has been a godsend to the *Adventures of Dusty Sourdough*. The professionalism of Evan Swensen and his staff are unequaled. As a writer I believe there isn't a better, more honest publisher anywhere. I recommend Publications Consultants to new writers as well as to veterans. Glen Guy: *A Gift for Dusty, Trail To Wrangell, Adventure Gold, Adventure Fire*

As a first-time author I found Publication Consultants to be extremely helpful in getting me through the maze of the publishing game. Evan Swensen did an excellent job of transforming my photos and text into a readable and visually pleasing book. His patience and willingness to work with authors are to be commended. Joseph Kurtak: *Mine in the Sky*

Publication Consultants
PO Box 221974
Anchorage, Alaska 99522
Phone (907) 349-2424 Fax (907) 349-2426
books@publicationconsultants.com
www.publicationconsultants.com